THERE'S A CROWD

Jillian Powell
Illustrated by Terry Howell Stanley

Rigby
A Harcourt Achieve Imprint

www.Rigby.com
1-800-531-5015

Literacy by Design Leveled Readers: *Three's A Crowd*

ISBN-13: 978-1-4189-3783-6
ISBN-10: 1-4189-3783-5

Printed in China
1B 2 3 4 5 6 7 8 985 13 12 11 10 09 08 07

Grace's Diary
Don't look!

June 12
Dear Diary,

I'm so excited because there's only one more week until school is out! I can't wait for summer vacation. Last night I sang in the school concert. I wore my new dress, and Grandma helped me do my hair. I thought Dad looked a bit sad when I came downstairs. He said I looked just like Mom.

Tomorrow it will be two years since Mom died. I know because that's when I started this diary. Writing in a diary is a bit like talking to a really good friend.
Anyway, I gave Dad a big hug and told him how much fun we're going to have this summer, and how he and I (and Barney, our dog) make a great team.

June 17 ☆

Dear Diary, ⭐

Dad put up the basketball hoop next to the driveway today, so now I can practice shooting baskets all the time. I really want to be on the basketball team next year. Dad says if I work hard, I could be their top point scorer!

June 20
Dear Diary,

When Dad finished work today, we had a basket-shooting contest—and I won! Dad's going to take some time off this summer so we can do some fun things together. I teased him by saying I get to choose what we'll do. Dad says we'll vote on it—that means he puts up his hand, but I put up both my hands. Then he says, "OK, I'm outvoted!"

June 21
Dear Diary,

The thing I'm most looking
forward to this summer is finishing
my tree house. Here's what I want
it to look like. It'll be my own special
place, where I can sit and write in
you—my diary—and listen to my music.

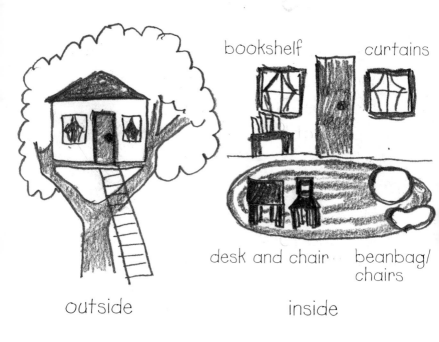

bookshelf   curtains

desk and chair   beanbag/
                                  chairs

outside   inside

Last weekend we started building the tree house in the backyard maple tree. The three big branches are perfect for holding it, and in the fall, the leaves are a brilliant blaze of orange, yellow, and red.

My job is to pass up pieces of wood and tools to Dad. Once it's done, I'll be able to see all around.

June 25
Dear Diary,

Dad got a letter from Aunt Irene saying she has to go to the hospital for an operation and will need time to heal. She asked if cousin Ricky could stay with us for the summer. Dad says it'll be fun having Ricky around, but I'm afraid our plans will change if he's here.

June 26
Dear Diary,

   Ricky's coming in three days, so
I helped get the spare room ready.
Dad wants to have a special dinner
when Ricky arrives. He says we
should help Ricky feel at home
because he'll be worried about
his mom. (I know what it's like to
worry about your mom.)

June 30
Dear Diary,

Ricky arrived yesterday. He's in eighth grade and thinks he's so smart. When I was shooting baskets today, he came up behind me, caught the ball, and made three baskets in a row. What a big show-off! He told me not to worry because he'd teach me everything he knows about hoops! He kept calling me Gracie. I told him that my name is Grace, not Gracie, but he just grinned.

July 1
Dear Diary,

    Ricky is so annoying. He whistles
to himself and drums his fingers on
his arms whether he's listening to
music or not! He teases poor Barney
by pretending he has a ball for him
to catch. Worst of all, he calls Dad
"Jack" as if they are best friends.
How rude!

July 2
Dear Diary,

It's only 8:00 p.m. and I'm ready to
say goodnight! Why? Because Ricky
has taken over downstairs—that's
why. He's playing video games with
Dad, eating popcorn, and acting like
he owns the place. When I came in
from outside, he said, "Come join us,
Gracie!" as if it were his place to
invite me!

I wanted to watch television, but Dad gave me the look—the "be-more-sympathetic look." When I said I hated video games, Dad thought we should vote (I think Dad was secretly having fun playing video games, too). Of course they put their hands up, and I was outvoted. With Ricky around, I'll never win. It's so unfair!

July 3
Dear Diary,

I must remember to hide my diary. Ricky saw it on my desk this morning and picked it up. For one awful moment, I thought he was going to read it! When he asked me why I keep a diary, I shouted at him to put it down and to keep away from my private things. Oh, he makes me so angry!

My best friend, Teri, came over today to show me her cool new camera. We were figuring out how to record short videos on it when Ricky came in and said he'd show us how to play the videos back on the computer. Teri thinks he's really smart. Now he's even taking over my friends!

July 5
Dear Diary,

This morning I heard Dad and Ricky talking downstairs. I heard Ricky say, "I can help you build it." Then Dad said, "Well, that's our project for the summer then." Our project—the tree house was supposed to be MY project with Dad. I was so upset, I stormed out of the house, slamming the door behind me!

outside

July 6
Dear Diary,

Dad wasn't happy with me for slamming the door last night. He said I was being unkind to Ricky. I said I was sorry and reminded him that he and I were going to build the tree house together—not him and Ricky!

Dad explained that they hadn't been talking about the tree house. Instead, Dad said the two of them had a great idea to build kayaks! Apparently, Ricky and Dad saw kayak kits on the Internet. They're going to build them in the backyard, and then we'll go river running together. (Three guesses whose idea that was!)

July 15
Dear Diary,

Dad and Ricky have started building the kayaks, and I feel useless. When I told Ricky that Dad and I already had a summer project—my tree house—he said, "Gracie, you only have one view from a tree house, but in a kayak, you get to see a million views!"

July 27
Dear Diary,

All Dad and Ricky talk about
is kayaks, kayaks, kayaks! It's so
boring, but today I helped them
stretch the skins over the frames.
I must admit, those weird skeletons
are starting to look like boats. But
I still got annoyed when know-it-all
Ricky said, "Just imagine, Gracie,
soon you'll be paddling a kayak you
helped to build." He acts SO superior!

August 1

Dear Diary,

Today we went for a kayaking lesson. We learned how to get in and out of the kayak safely, how to paddle and turn, and how to do a stroke called a "brace," which steadies the kayak if it starts to tip. Ricky's done this before, so he made it look easy. He showed how to do a roll if you turn over—what a show-off!!

August 9
Dear Diary,

Kayaking is HARD, especially when my kayak seems to have a mind of its own. I can nearly steer a straight course, but when I try to turn, I feel like I'm going to tip over! Dad wants to go kayaking on the river tomorrow. I'm nervous and don't want to go, but Ricky told me to remember the paddlers' rule—less than three there should never be.

August 10
Dear Diary,

Today we took the kayaks on the river for the first time. It was a beautiful day, and the water sparkled. At first I felt scared because I thought I was going to tip over, but Ricky stayed alongside me and gave me directions. (I suppose sometimes he can be useful!)

August 16
Dear Diary,

OK, I give up. Our kayaking trip yesterday was a BLAST, and I can't wait to go again! Most of the time, all I could hear was the steady *dib-dab* of the paddles on the peaceful river. Sometimes I could hear a fish jumping effortlessly in and out of the water.

August 22
Dear Diary,

Yesterday we were out river running again, and I'm still in shock. Dad was ahead, Ricky was behind him, and I was following Ricky. The river was high because it had rained a lot. Suddenly, Ricky shouted. Then I saw this log sticking out of the water, and then Dad's kayak turned over. It all happened so fast!

Ricky shouted for me to get to
the riverbank and find help while he
paddled madly toward Dad's kayak.
I got to the bank and ran and ran.
I finally found some people fishing
and was thankful when one of them
called for help on his cell phone.
When I got back, Dad was on the
bank, wet as an otter, and coughing
up river water. Ricky had saved
Dad's life!

August 23
Dear Diary,

Grandma is looking after Ricky and me while Dad is in the hospital. The doctor says he's fine and will be home in a few days—thanks to Ricky! The images of Dad's upturned kayak and my scramble to find help just keep replaying in my head.

Dad says it was an accident. Even though the river is tame, currents can get stronger and faster when they flow around things in their path. After Dad hit the log, the current turned him over and over. Dad said he felt like he was in a washing machine. How Ricky stayed so calm, I don't know, but now he's my hero.

August 24
Dear Diary,

Today after Ricky and I took
Barney out for a walk, we sat under
the maple tree and talked for hours.
He told me how worried he is about
his mom. So I told him how I still miss
my mom, but I try to remember all
the happy times we had together.
I'm so grateful for each memory.

August 25
Dear Diary,

    It rained all day, so we stayed in and Ricky showed me how to draw a Gratitude Tree. First you draw a root for each person who has died but loved you in the past. Then you draw a branch for each person who loves you now. Then you draw a leaf for each of the things you love in your life. I decided to put Ricky's visit on one of my leaves.

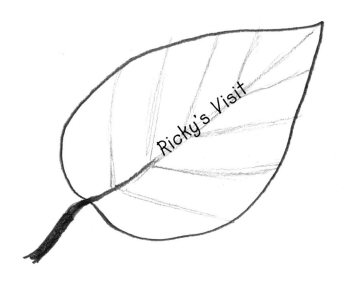

August 26
Dear Diary,

I can't believe how quickly the summer has gone. Dad's back home, and he's doing fine. Ricky's *mom* is also doing well. Tonight we had a farewell barbecue for Ricky. We sat outside on the kayaks and talked and ate under the stars. It was a great evening, and I realized how much I'm going to miss Ricky.

August 28
Dear Diary,

Ricky left today! Yesterday he painted names on our kayaks. Mine is called Gracie. I guess I can live with that! Ricky asked if he can come again next summer and help us work on my tree house. Dad and I voted the same—YES! I can't wait!

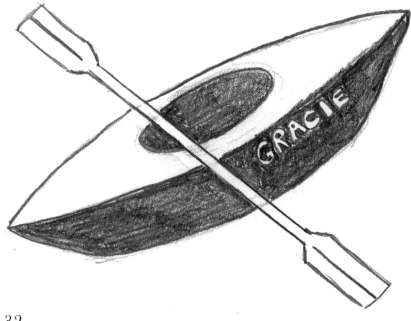